James Daniel Lynch

Robert E. Lee

Or, Heroes of the South

James Daniel Lynch

Robert E. Lee
Or, Heroes of the South

ISBN/EAN: 9783337193881

Printed in Europe, USA, Canada, Australia, Japan

Cover: Foto ©Thomas Meinert / pixelio.de

More available books at **www.hansebooks.com**

Robert E. Lee,

OR,

HEROES OF THE SOUTH.

A POEM.

BY

JAMES D. LYNCH

WEST POINT, MISS.:
George R. Carr, Book and Job Printer.
1876.

ROBERT E. LEE,

OR,

Heroes of the South.

CANTO I.

SUMMARIUM.

Invocation to Truth—Lincoln, President of the United States—His policy towards the South—The assembling of the Southern armies—The "On to Richmond"—General Lee arrives in Richmond, and is placed in command—The armies engage in terrible conflict—Mr. Davis secretly sends Lee to ask succor of Victoria, queen of England—The hero, together with Mason, sets sail—He is overtaken by a terrible tempest caused by the Furies of Puritan—He lands on an island, where an old Revolutionary soldier predicts to him his fate, and, conditionally, that of his country.

PROEMIUM.

Aid me O Muse! while I, in reckless flight,
Attempt the pathway, and the tow'ring hight
Of those, whose genius wrapt in dazzling maze,
Doth scorch the wings that flutter round its blaze :
Of its bright visions grant me to partake,
Or ease my fate for honest effort's sake.

Of heroes of the Southern land I sing,
As brave as ever fought for right or king,
Or Roman lance or Spartan armor wore,
Or ever trod the Hellespontic shore:
And they had learned in noble valor's school,
Themselves to govern and mankind to rule :
To hold their birthright and their faith maintain,
They nobly sacrificed their all, in vain.

Descend O Truth! from thy celestial hight,
And shed upon my song thy brightest light;
Let thy pure voice the ears of rulers reach,
Thy precepts warn them and examples teach;
Thou should'st announce to them what they should know,
What grief and sorrow from their follies flow;
Should'st teach them peace, and spread before their eyes,
The woe and mischief that from wars arise.
Oh! say to me if true that fable old,
With thy proud voice its thrilling legends told;
If its weak feet can climb thy lofty hight,
Its shade adorn the glances of thy light;
Then let it go with me, thou being guide,
To ornament thy charms and not to hide.

A man was seated in the Nation's chair,
Whom sectional hate and vengeance had placed there:
The reins of state were galling in his hands,
And threatened ruin to the Southern lands.
Our Magna Charta and our country's pride,
Was folded up and rudely thrust aside;
The laws were unenforced, all right ignored,
And Heaven then no longer was adored.
But vengeance dire usurped the place of law,
And waved the sword of bloody civil war.
Our country bore no more the honored name
Of "Land of Liberty" and peaceful fame,
Whose path so prosperous in freedom's ways,
Had made all Europe with pale terror gaze.
But now, its dazzling glory was all passed,
And its first rank was clouded by its last.
Can such debasement from one wrong act spring,
And cherished name become a hateful thing?
But Patience has a borne to her control,
Beyond, oppression's waves can never roll

In safety, not safe hand its current guide,
And pathway open for its fatal tide.

Enthroned he sat, the king of sectional hate,
His ill-got rank disposed the scales of fate:
Around him flocked fierce ministers of woe,
There CHASE and STANTON and revengeful GROW,
And high-law SEWARD and exponent BATES,
Devised the ruin of the Southern States;
Preceptors, who his peaceful aims annulled,
They roused his vengeance and his virtues lulled.
And LINCOLN now assumed despotic rank,
And rose his grandeur as his country's sank.
In Washington was formed the Union League,
The nurse of crime and monster of intrigue.
The Southern people all his plans foresaw,
And threw their banners to the gales of war,
Which now swept fiercely over all the land,
From the Ohio to the Texan strand:
The grim clouds gathered on Virginia's coast,
There met the Southrons and the Northern host:
Along Potomac's fairy banks they burst,
Which ne'er before had quench'd the soldier's thirst.

Now, to revolted Richmond came a man,
The scene grew red when LEE his work began.
Brave, virtuous LEE, and full of sanguine fight,
Came to his people to restore the light:
He roused their spirit, showed to them the way
From shame to glory, and rebuked dismay.
His noble State had stepped within the breach,
To shield her sisters from invasion's reach;
Had bared her bosom to the strokes of war,
Her honor bade her and that was her law;

Determined to protect or with them fall,
The bulwark and the champion of them all.
And in his hands she placed her honored sword,
To keep it bright he pledged his sacred word;
And well did he that solemn pledge redeem,
That sword was worn and sheathed in honor's gleam.
So soon as known to Richmond he had gone,
Abe Lincoln trembled and Scott was forlorn.

From Richmond westward near the flowery verge,
Where pours the James its wild meandering surge;
Now, places charming, pleasant, pure retreats,
Where arts rejoice and nature strows her sweets,
Were scenes of bustle then, and war's alarms,
Heroic Lee had gathered here his arms.
Here heroes, proud props of their country, came,
In faith divided but in cause the same;
To his safe hands they now commit their fate,
He gains their hearts, their hopes become elate.
The hero's father, peering from the skies,
Beheld the glory of his lineage rise;
Foresaw the glory he himself desired,
The rank he envied and his son admired.
Old Light-Horse from on high his help accords,
And all unseen, his strength'ning arm affords;
For fear the hero with success inspired,
The danger less, less glory had acquired.

In Washington, the world wild vengeance saw,
Inciting Lincoln and the League to war:
Both church and state, allied in wrathful strains,
Invoking ruin on the Southern plains.
Old "Fuss and Feathers" with his motley band,
Of variegated hues from every land,

With fire and sword to lay waste hill and dell,
Now onward came "To Richmond or to hell:"
He Winfield called, the traitor and the foe
To his own people sunk in hopeless woe,
Now came to plunder his ancestral lands,
With blood of kindred, came to stain his hands.
He thought that nothing could his march retard,
Until he Johnston met and Beauregard.
The armies in their bloody work engaged,
And more than once a dreadful combat waged.
The demon carnage, wandered through the fields;
From sea to sea resounded swords and shields.
The Southern soldiers bore the victor's crown,
Till grim exhaustion weighed their efforts down.

And Davis, now by countless ills oppressed,
In solemn strains, the hero thus addressed:
Oh! Lee, behold against what odds we fight,
Must we contend against the whole world's might?
Religion, dreadful in its wrath and hate,
Its fierce anath'mas hurls against our state.
And slander too, has played its wonted part,
And 'gainst our cause has turned all Europe's heart.
And while our losses are repaired no more,
Their pleth'ric ranks are filled from every shore.
Against so many foes so odd our chance,
We must seek aid of England or of France.
Let us engage in secret England's queen,
I know, against our cause, a mortal spleen
Will hardly suffer us to be allied,
Our forms of government have always vied:
And while our glory is exposed to shame,
We neither friends nor government can claim.
See how with fire and sword they sweep our plains,
And what we lose the greedy Yankee gains.

While wishing us avowedly to confuse,
He hates our people and their wealth pursues.
I crave the grim marauders to chastise,
Who us avenges are friends in my eyes.
In such an office I will not employ
A common agent or a crude envoy:
But you alone, you whose sagacious sense,
Alone, can kings engage in our defense:
To Britain go, and in vehement strain
There plead our cause, and arms for us obtain:
Through you I wish our foes to dispossess,
And hope for aid, alone through your address.
He said: The hero, jealous of his name,
Would not forego the prospect of such fame;
But list'ning, felt deep grief and sorrow's dart,
When he remember'd times dear to his heart;
When with his arms alone, without intrigue,
He had defeated and confused the League:
Though trammell'd by the President's commands,
His blows were parried, yet it felt his hands.
And leaving laurels, now new pluck'd, behind,
To leave these scenes he was resolved in mind.
The soldiers nothing knew of his intent,
Of his return all waited the event:
He goes, yet Washington's scared populace,
Expects him still to fall on them apace.
His name, his country's pillow and proud stay,
Inspires fear while he is far away.
And now he moved across Virginia's plain,
With none but MASON of his faithful train;
His trusty friend, in whom he could confide,
For he was never seen on error's side:
With signal zeal and elevated thought,
For right and justice, he had always fought;
In upright purpose and in learned debate,
He added honor to his native State.

6

Where now between two cliffs the rolling deep,
Hurls back its waves against the stony steep,
From Norfolk's port, they with propitious gales
Embark'd, the ardent sailors trim the sails:
The ship, proud sov'reign of the mighty main,
Was ready now to plow the wat'ry plain;
The north winds fast to upper regions bound,
To the mild zephyrs left the vast profound.
The anchor weigh'd, they dash'd forth from the land,
Their course was bound for England's distant strand.

But hatred, demon of our country's grief,
Watch'd their departure and espied the chief:
And straightway then to Plymouth rock she went,
With bosom heaving and on mischief bent:
There sat her father, Puritan of old,
To nations long the source of grief untold;
His children 'round him in obeisance wait,
There, greed and envy and religious hate,
Are by psalm-singing saints and preachers taught;
By moral preachers of the BEECHER sort.
While father Puritan above them sat,
With hair cropp'd short and sugar-loaf shaped hat,
And nose far-peering, and spectacled eyes,
In all mankinds affairs he peeps and pries.
Said hatred then, in melancholic strain,
A hero, father, sails upon the main;
While crouching lately near the Ches'peake's mouth,
I saw embark the Hero of the South:
To England's strand his direct course was bent,
No doubt on mischief and some dire intent.
Thus, Puritan the sable throng addressed,
Who eager list'ning, round their monarch pressed;
Revenge, hate, envy, woe and furies all,
And subjects heedful to your sovereign's call:

The chief foe of my kingdom and of me,
Now makes his way across the eastern sea:
Go; speed away, his ship upset or bring
Him bound in chains, a prisoner to your king.
The furies darted forth and with broad sweep,
And foaming rage, they hovered o'er the deep:
Then suddenly, the skies became obscured,
The howling winds blew fierce, the deep sea roared;
The dazzling light'ning glitter'd in the clouds,
Now, wave on wave and billow billow crowds:
And the hoarse thunder growling from afar,
New horror added to the tempest war:
Below, the yawning deep, above, the skies,
Present but death to the pale sailors' eyes.
Not fiercer, thus did Juno's vengeance urge,
The angry winds, and heave the Tuscan surge
Around Æneas, eager to destroy
The only vestige and remains of Troy.

The hero cased in danger was not moved,
But for his people and the land he loved:
And thither turned his eyes and his great mind,
Seemed only to deplore the hostile wind.
Less sanguine, thus great Cæsar near Epire,
When he disputed there the world's empire,
Entrusted to the sea by tempest whirl'd,
The fate of Rome and of the Roman world:
Defying Pompey and Old Neptune's might,
Oppos'd his fortune to the double fight.

But at this moment the creation's God,
Who rides upon the winds and heaves the flood;
That God, whose wisdom, pow'r and strength untold,
Did raise up Rome and throw down Troy of old;

From his bright throne that glitters in the skies,
On the great hero deigned to cast his eyes;
And guided him, the storm by his command,
The vessel wafted to the nearest land;
Where islands from the ocean seemed to rise,
The hero landed, aided by the skies.
Close by the shore a woodland's dark retreat,
Its shade afforded, an asylum sweet:
A rock between it and the sea arose,
From wind and wave protecting its repose.
A cave was near, whose rough interior part,
Disclaimed itself to be the work of art.
An aged man, far from the scenes of strife,
Had sought this place to pass a quiet life;
Far from the bustling crowd to man unknown,
Here, in deep solitude, he lived alone;
Here, he reflected on his useless days,
Days spent in pleasure and in sinful ways.
Along the grassy meads and fountain's side,
Beneath his feet he trod all human pride,
And calmly waited for the time to come,
When God would take him to his final home:
The God he served supported his old age,
And in this desert he became a sage;
By gift Divine, became in mystery wise,
The book of fate was opened to his eyes.
The old man knew the hero from a dream,
And spread refreshments near a limpid stream.
The chief these rude repasts had oft enjoy'd,
And often when by bustling scenes annoy'd,
To some old soldier's roof had fled, and there
Threw down the burden of official care.
The sad condition of their native State,
Afforded ample subject for debate;

The hero, in deep founded faith, unmov'd,
A firm believer in secession proved.
The old man doubting, called for, from the skies
Some brighter light to shine upon his eyes:
At all times, said he, Truth is pure and fixed,
While human efforts are with error mixed.
Then, said the chief, shall I not know the way
Of Truth, on which alone my hopes must stay?
God sometimes, said the old man, hides his face,
But to rebuke the wayward human race:
I have ere this beheld oppression's hand,
Extended high above our native land,
And proudly seated on a mighty throne,
There stretch with scornful foot our birthright prone.
And then, as if from regions of the dead,
Young Freedom raise again its fearless head,
And grapple with the foe until, at length,
The despot crouched beneath its growing strength.
Our noble State beheld the final scene,
Oppression's arms were stacked upon her green;
The pearly James bore to its ocean bed,
The last blood washed from freedom's gory head;
Its waves still murmur the oppressor's knell,
As it rolls onward through its flow'ry dell:
Nor sweeter, thus the songster's sad remains,
From Hebrus' tide prolonged his dying strains,
And Old Anchyta's shade in barren sands,
The burial service begged from sailors' hands.

A dark scene then appeared before my eyes,
I saw the Puritanic furies rise;
Far from their reach to this lone cave obscure,
I came my country's ruin to deplore;
Where Hope, perhaps, might soothe my latter days,
Such creeds and isms can not last always.

From human caprice they derived their birth,
Like it will perish and return to earth;
All wicked schemes of men soon pass away,
God scatters them with truth's enlight'ning ray.
He is a unit, while the world is rife,
With creeds and sects engaged in endless strife.
Truth dwells at the eternal feet divine,
And rarely doth upon poor mortals shine;
Who seeks it with his heart will one day see,
You shall be wakened since you wish to be.
The hand of God will guide you through the war,
Yet be not sanguine nor too hopeful, for
Unless bright truth shall bound your effort's scope,
To enter Washington you must not hope.
To you his voice proclaims the hero's meads,
And the road opens which to glory leads.
When after battles horrible with blood,
Your country shall afford its army food,
Then will its grief and pains be at an end,
And sorrow's hand no more your heart shall rend.
To God, then, you will lift your thankful eyes,
The God of battles who dwells in the skies;
And know, the true heart may in Him confide,
Go; serve Him, and He will your footsteps guide.

He ceased, each word was like a flaming dart,
That pierced the bottom of the hero's heart,
He felt transported to that primal age,
When God talked with the reverential sage;
When simple virtue was of mighty worth,
Commanded kings, and oracles drew forth.
With deep regret he left the reverend seer,
Embracing him, he shed the parting tear,
And from that moment glimps'd the lurid morn,
Of that dark day of woe so soon to dawn.

The old man thus, instructed by his Lord,
Addressed the chief and touched his tender chord.
His sacred words the boisterous winds appease,
The sun appeared and calm became the seas:
The chief then leading to the placid main,
He bade him safely speed to Britain's plain.

CANTO II.

SUMMARIUM.

The hero arrives in England—Description of the state of the country—
He has an interview with the Queen, and, at her request, relates to her
the causes of the war between the States—She is disposed to aid the
South—Gladstone opposes, and the hero's mission fails—He returns
home—He runs the blockade and arrives at Charleston—Repairs to Virginia—Engages Grant at the Wilderness—The "Overland Campaign"—
Misses Stonewall Jackson—Siege of Richmond and Petersburg—The
hero's lines are broken—His retreat and surrender at Appommattox.

In England, now, they secretly admire,
The happy changes of that vast empire,
Where constant breaches of the wisest laws,
Was long to prince and state the sorrow's cause.
Now, on the scene where countless heroes died,
The throne a hundred kings had occupied,
A woman sat, and at her feet lay fate,
The world admired the greatness of her state.
It was VICTORIA, whose sagacious skill,
Made Europe yield its balance to her will;
And the proud English loved her yoke to wear,
Who can nor servitude nor freedom bear.

Her subjects little felt their golden chains,
Full were their barns and plenty strewed their plains;
Flocks fill'd their meads and vessels lined their strand;
Lords of the sea and feared upon the land.
Ah! cried the chief, when shall my country be,
Like this, from savage war and rapine free?
Oh! what a lesson, rulers of the world,
A woman has of war the banner furled;
Has shut and barred grim Janus' temple door,
And fury whets her rusting arms no more.
'Tis happy, when a people duty taught,
Respect the sovereign power as it ought;
More happy, when a ruler just and good,
Respects the people's welfare as he should;
For Peace will shed her beams upon that land,
And plenty's heavy laden wings expand.
To London now they came, the world's great mart,
And Mars' stern temple and the queen of art;
Here they beheld the Norman victor's tower,
Near by VICTORIA had her royal bower.
The hero then, with MASON, sought the queen,
And found her free from all that pomp and sheen,
From which the great are rarely e'er exempt,
But which true heroes look on with contempt.
The listening queen he plies in earnest strains,
And plenally his country's wants explains:
Although extremely painful to his heart,
With much decorum he performed his part.
"Are you that LEE," inquired the royal dame,
Whose deeds bedeck the firmament of fame,
Is he the peer of all distinguished names,
Here as an envoy on the banks of Thames?
To seek my succor and my friendship gain,
How could they spare you from Virginia's plain?

From rising sun to where it couches down,
Your great achievements are of world renown.
You, who so many brilliant fights have made,
Why do you think of asking foreign aid?
Misfortune, Madam, stifles my disdains,
I think now only of my country's chains.
You can great queen along this road to fame,
Forever carve your own and England's name;
To crown your virtues and our freedom gain,
Come help us and we will fast friends remain.

The queen demanded first that he relate,
The story of the troubles in his State.
What combination such events could bring,
And from what sources could such actions spring;
What circumstances marvellous and strange,
In the great Union had produced such change;
Already, said she, whispers of report,
These sanguine scenes have pictured at my court;
Its dual tongue anon both sides defends,
And no doubt often truth with falsehood blends:
Its fab'lous tales I always half reject,
You can relieve all doubts in this respect;
A hero, surely, can the best depict,
The real scenes of his own great conflict.
Explain to me these changes in your state,
Which you alone are worthy to relate;
Tell all, the happy and unhappy things,
Your deeds can teach a lesson to all kings.
Alas! the hero said, must I review,
And in my mem'ry these sad scenes renew?
Would that forgetfulness the task would save,
And drown remembrance in dark Lethe's wave:
But truth lives on and never can decay,
And you command me and I will obey:

Relating them, one might without surprise,
The bright discover and the dark disguise;
Such subtle artifice I do abhor,
I speak the soldier not embassador.

   The queen was silent and with calm intent,
Her eager gaze upon the hero bent,
And glancing downward, then the modest man,
Arranged his posture and his theme began:
The story's long and ere my task be done,
Time will have sped a whole revolving sun;
But if your patience lends a listening ear,
My people's wrongs and suff'rings you shall hear.
This mighty conflict, Madam, took its rise,
Beneath your happy but once troubled skies:
The Roundheads here began their bloody strife,
Which made your kingdom tremble for its life;
The same once caused your people's blood to pour
In streams at Naseby and Marston-Moor.
Exiled from here, they straight to Holland sped,
And there new treasons and new troubles bred.
New England next beheld their gloomy fleet,
On Plymouth rock they placed their blighting feet;
There passed their time in melancholly rites,
In hearing voices and in seeing sights,
In saintly trances, swoons and fainting qualms,
In burning witches and in singing psalms.
And here old Puritan his rule began,
In garb of Heaven, yet a foe to man:
And when all fixed religion felt its hate,
It sought to ruin or control the state.
Then from the bleak, cold regions of the North,
All kinds of isms and new creeds poured forth;
Here envy, sectional hate and strife were bred,
Whose sable wings soon o'er our country spread.

Far southward thence, its ancient foe it spied;
The Cavaliers had throng'd the Chesapeake's tide;
The arts and wealth had followed their advance;
There, rang the axe and gleamed the knightly lance.
A mutual trouble called for mutual aid,
And thus, between them was alliance made.
Your fathers erred, against their cruel laws,
A common sword we drew in freedom's cause.
Such union, Madam, no less could create,
Than self-defense or stern decree of fate.
Within the vitals of our country's life,
There lurked the causes of this bloody strife.
The generous Cavalier and Huguenot,
Could not by the grim Puritan be taught,
To deem him Heaven's chosen and elect,
To whom all men must cringe with dumb respect.
And then began their mischief and intrigue,
The Union was proclaimed a lasting league;
Yet every sacred feature was infringed,
On which the contract and the Union hinged.
Protective tariff was the primal stroke,
To place the Southern people under yoke;
Then down with slavery was the "hue and cry,"
Although these slaves they urged the South to buy;
When they were without profit at the North,
They sold them at the South for their full worth.

Then a provision, baseless and unwise,
Was made and called "Missouri Compromise;"
Without one feature reason could define,
'Twas fixed alone on geographic line,
Which either party might o'erstep at will;
Then came the Kansas and Nebraska bill,
When, squatter sovereign doctrine and free-soil,
Again our country kept in fierce turmoil.

Now, LINCOLN grasped the galling reins of state,
On platform breathing sectional strife and hate;
The South within fixed limits to restrain,
And bar her from the national domain.
The Constitution which protected all,
Was trampled down, and in its place the pall
Of painted isms, called the "Higher Law,"
Spread o'er our country one dark scene of war.
Throughout the North, from Maine to Illinois,
Seemed but one wish, the Southrons to destroy.
Less eager, thus the Persian's countless bands,
Were bent on ruin of the Grecian lands:
And fierce Crusader craved with pious heart,
The blood of Infidel upon his dart:
In streams they pour'd from northern vale and hill,.
Their lands to lay waste and the Southrons kill.
As Kansas hoppers on their vernal tour,
In cloudy swarms their greedy legions pour,
So came the Northern arms in maddened rush,
The South to humble and rebellion crush.
Virginia called me and at her command,
I drew my sword for her, my native land.
But why should I prolong this tale of woe,
The causes you have heard, the rest you know.
Shall arms successful on the hard fought field,
To gaunt starvation and exhaustion yield?
But ample staple we have still for trade,
If you great Queen will break the false blockade;
And then no tariff shall between us be,
Your trade with us shall be forever free.

The queen was mov'd and mildly thus replied,
My heart, Sir Chief, is with your cause allied;
And armies should be, could I act alone,
I must consult with DERBY and GLADSTONE.

And she her council board convoked, and then,
Addressed them thus, "My Lords and Gentlemen:"
The question I prefer for your debates,
Is peace or war with the United States.
From its great hero and its chieftain's mouth,
I 've heard the wrongs and suff'rings of the South:
My heart is always with the cause of right,
Contending with brute force and numbers might:
Why may we not at once by armed decree,
Arrest this conflict and the South set free;
Or else, at least, for sake of vital trade,
Ignore and break the paper made blockade?

But the great Premier, whose frigid heart,
Could never from cold selfish views depart;
And with deep schemes of politics inlaid,
This counsel rendered and this answer made:
The blockade, Madam, will in war's event,
To us afford a valued precedent;
With our strong ships alligned along their shore,
The Paris treaty will bind us no more:
And let them tear each other as they'choose,
We gain new power and strong rivals lose;
And while their fields are covered with their slain,
Our Canadas are safe, this much we gain.
Besides, the issue we have oft foretold,
The great Republic goes like those of old.
To each let us full right of war accord,
To neither side or arms or aid afford;
And not transcend the bounds of nations' law,
Unless to foster and prolong the war.

The hero with regret, his mission vain,
Now homeward sped his way across the main.

Where Ireland's sea enfroths its foaming tide,
Against the rugged cliffs far up the Clyde,
At port of Glasgow, there the hero shipped,
The vessel through the northern channel skipped;
And soon the Giant's causeway paled from view,
While they across the world of waters flew.
Full twenty days their varied course had run,
And when the twenty-first revolving sun,
Was brightly peeping from its ocean bed,
The seas were calm and blue the vault o'erhead;
Along the margin of the sea girt skies,
A verdant shore from ocean seemed to rise:
Now hostile sails across their leaway loom'd,
And suddenly a distant cannon boom'd.
For near the Carolina's hated coast,
Had gathered thickly the blockading host:
The armless vessel, girded for the chase,
While mail clad war ships urg'd the rapid chase;
The space between them narrowed as they sped,
While messengers of death leaped o'er their head.
But lo! the walls of Sumpter frown'd in view,
And the pursuers from the chase withdrew:
A hundred port holes on her walls were clear'd,
A hundred guns upon the foe were veered;
A vengeful missile through their rigging crash'd,
And far beyond the foaming waters lash'd.
The hero now rode safely into port,
Beneath the ramparts of the famous fort;
On shore, he straightway to Virginia hied,
And plung'd again in battles crimson tide.

There GRANT, now leader of the Northern host,
Came onward with great pomp and waggish boast;
That he in Richmond on the Fourth would dine,
Or fight all summer on his chosen line.

But in the Wilderness his hopes were sear'd,
And his straight line was to the northward veer'd;
And then once more, from Spotsylvania's plain,
The braggart chieftain swung around again;
Like some shy cur when by a mastiff bit,
Again him meeting will the pathway quit;
Thus, he around the fatal circle rolled,
With losses greater than LEE's arms all told.
His hammering process proved a slaughter-pen,
That cost him more than sixty thousand men.

And now the hero missed that man of might,
His hope in council and right arm in fight:
Who thundered on the Young Napoleon's flank,
And to JOE HOOKER gave that fatal spank:
O Chancellorville! what ill luck marr'd thy plains,
And turn'd the victors' shouts to mourning strains;
That fatal bullet whizz'd a nation's knell,
On that dark day when STONEWALL JACKSON fell.
The sea unfolds its treasures now and then,
The earth its precious jewels bright and rare,
While fame's illumin'd scroll of noted men,
But seldom shows so pure and brilliant star.
He was a man in deed, whose lofty aim,
Involved no selfish thought or love of fame;
But well and truly to perform his part,
His country's weal was deepest in his heart:
And where the fiercest tides of battle rolled,
"Press forward men!" a tale of carnage told.

Now what McCLELLAND vainly tried before,
GRANT gladly sought, the capitol's back door;
But there Cold Harbor's field the lesson taught,
That his advance must by the spade be wrought:

And Northern patience taxed with further time,
E're Richmond's fall the northern bells could chime.
Yet winding ditches and exploding mines,
Made no impression on the hero's lines;
Which lay unmov'd with bristling front arrayed,
Before the city, calm and undismayed.
And like a maddened lion he stood there,
Or wounded tigress in her mountain lair;
While GRANT abandon'd all direct attack,
And to the war clad city turned his back:
Far southward now his serried columns reach,
In search of some weak point or easy breach;
But find the hero's ranks in front conjoint,
And BUTLER "bottled up" at City Point.

There is a limit to all human skill,
In contest 'twixt brute force and valor's will;
Time, when the weak before the strong must fall,
As giant mountains overtop the small:
Though one contain but common earth and stone,
While precious jewels deck the smaller cone.
The hero had foreseen the fatal stroke,
His slender line was stretch'd until it broke.
When darkness now had veil'd the vaulted arch,
His sleepless troops were gather'd for the march:
From line of battle, trench and ramparts' hight,
The army came forth in the gloom of night;
While bursting shells and loud exploding mines,
Convulsed the earth along the vacant lines;
Mid fiery pillows, promptly it obeyed
Its chieftain's voice, unmoved and undismayed.

And when Aurora blushed the crimson dawn,
And shot her beams along the dewy lawn,

A pall of smoke was seen above the James,
And Richmond was involved in rolling flames:
Along the margin of the fiery sea,
Now poured the foe in wild exulting glee;
With glist'ning muskets and victorious shouts,
They seized the city and its dumb redoubts.
While, far to westward, through the morning spray,
The hero's army wound its weary way;
But ever and anon it turned its eyes,
To the dark cloud that drap'd the eastern skies.
The sun lit forest with its sparkling sheen,
Mock splendor added to the novel scene;
Anon, by day, fierce troopers on them dash'd,
While all night long bright signal torches flash'd.
The citizens with dumb dismay were shocked,
While the deep forest with explosions rocked.
And now began new horrors and untold,
Or ever felt in modern times or old;
Food! food! became a starving army's cry:
And brave and fearless men laid down to die;
Men whom fierce battle's tide had lashed in vain,
Now gladly sought a place among the slain.
The hero strove against this to provide,
But his wise orders had been set aside.
Meantime the army with its remnant trains,
Was now approaching Appomattox' plains:
While on the march the army struggled here,
A fierce attack was made upon its rear;
The foe repulsed, the bitter lesson learned,
That yet the hero's battle fires burned:
His army nobly played its final game,
And carved new niches on the shafts of fame.

And now the Ninth of April, solemn day,
Found the great hero at defiant bey;

With gallant GORDON arming in the van,
To die or cut through to the James or Dan;
Lo! What a scene! Two thousand famished men,
Resolved on cutting through ten thousand ten.
But pity's eye looked down from Heaven's vault,
And all humanity proclaimed a halt.
The guns were hushed and ere the setting sun,
Were placed in stack, the hero's work was done.

CANTO III.

SUMMARIUM.

The hero takes leave of his army—Retires to Richmond—His reception by
the citizens—Lives in seclusion—Infamous attempt of a Federal Judge
to cause his arrest for treason—Is called forth from his retirement—Be-
comes President of a College—His Death—The Radical Party continues
to persecute the South—Its ruinous policy—The situation of the sur-
vivors contrasted with the glory of the dead—A. S. Johnston—Polk—
Zollicoffer—McCullough—Cleburn—Stewart—Hill—The rebel dead.

Thus passed the great historical event,
The sun went down, a nation's life was spent;
Its life was measured by the cannon's boom,
Their silence marked its melancholly doom;
From them it drew its breath, with them it ceased,
And ruin was the remnant of its feast.
No thrilling diapason closed the scene,
But all beheld with calm and solemn mein;
The captives stacked their arms with measur'd tread,
Like mourners bearing to the tomb their dead:
No taunting shouts upon their senses jarred,
The foe respected and their feelings spared;
And now each soldier of that noble band,
But wished to shake the chieftain's parting hand;
To hear his well known voice again once more,
So often heard amid the cannon's roar:
In eager crowds they gathered 'round his tent,
And war worn veterans to their grief gave vent.
Then, thus the hero, with deep cast of thought,
Together men we through the war have fought,

I go submissive to what Heaven willed,
And you, with sense of duty well fulfilled;
And now, farewell, I've done my best for you,
My heart's too full, I can't say more, adieu.

    The hero slowly from the scene retired,
By foes esteemed, and by the world admired.
Paroled, at once he sought his quiet home,
To wait the issues and events to come.
It grieved him sorely from his troops to part,
Yet other troubles weighed upon his heart:
His country's future draped in deepest gloom,
New horror added to its settled doom.
And Richmond reached, he sought without display,
His house to enter by some private way.
But lo: the people thronged along the street,
Once more to welcome, and their hero greet.
He had so often passed along those ways,
The star of hope and admiration's gaze:
And the loud cheering of the people proved,
That they admired still, and still they loved.
Nor did the foe gainsay this deep applause,
This last ovation to their fallen cause:
But brave and noble men who wore the blue,
Their caps high raised in admiration too.
The chief no sign of recognition made,
Besides to raise his hat, no word he said;
Within his doors, again the curtain falls,
He shut himself within his mansion walls.
But that low malice which pursues defeat,
Its way soon wended to his calm retreat;
That modern Jeffries with his legal sword,
Now feign would cut the soldier's plighted word,
And brand with treason and the ban of law,
A man who wore the honor's crown of war.

25

But nobler sentiment around him stood,
And warded off the shafts of Underwood.

And now, once more, at duty's call he came,
And in new fields of honor carved his name.
Few could so well conduct the feet of youth,
In paths of honor, piety and truth:
For these are soonest from example caught,
His life itself the noble lesson taught.
But hark! did you not hear that solemn bell,
That tolling tocsin, that slow measur'd knell?
What tidings caus'd those solemn crowds to meet?
And why those pall drap'd banners o'er the street?
That common cast of grief and drooping head,
The hero, Robert Edward Lee, was dead.
The lightning flashed, the gloomy tidings sped,
And o'er the land a pall of sorrow spread.
And he had gone, his brave comrades to meet,
In Heaven's fields the true and brave to greet;
Who fell and never knew their country's fall,
Nor saw the ruin and the wreck of all:
They prized so highly and they loved so well,
Ah! happy they, who in hope's sunbeams fell.

'Tis sad from hopes that all the soul engage,
To fall, yet stand on beings barren stage:
A death of glory is the shining goal,
And crowning virtue of the noble soul.
More happy these, than those who did survive
Their country, and their cause and hope outlive;
Ah! they have pass'd through days as frought with gloom,
As ever marked the sable page of doom;
A harder fate no man of sense could have,
Than to be governed by his former slave.

But when grim Janus closed his temple door,
And hope's bright star was beaming forth once more:
If man had then the voice of hate eschewed,
Our country had her pleasant ways renewed.
But the disastrous mischief stopped not here,
For vengeance hovered in the battles' rear;
And ere the clouds of war had passed away,
While peace still struggled through the ling'ring spray;
Fierce hatred gathered up its gloomy might,
To crush the fallen and prolong the fight;
Though gorged with blood, 'twas not yet satiate,
For satisfaction is the death of hate.
But with new force new schemes of woe prepared,
And sought to ruin what the war had spared.
Not those who fought with clashing sword and shield,
In manly conflict on the equal field;
Brave men forbear, and when the fight is won,
Their arms are buried and their wrath is done.
But vengeance ever leads that dastard horde,
Who urge the conflict, yet they shun the sword;
And first upon the southern chiefs it burst,
And for no reason but that they were first
In rank, in fame and in their people's hearts,
The whole were chastised through the honor'd parts.
Great God! could not a mighty nation thrive,
And let an aged man in quiet live?
Whose only crime was that he dared to fill,
The place assigned him by a nation's will.
Those clanking chains! intended for his shame,
Left lasting stains upon Columbia's name.
His honor still survives all vengeance' powers,
And mid the ruins of his country towers:
Like some tall tree whose proud and giant form,
Still stands erect and weathers all the storm.

Fierce hordes of partisans were now alligned,
The South to humble and its people bind,
Fast to the axle of that party's car,
Which claimed its ruin as the spoil of war;
Which first proclaimed the Union was intact,
And yet promulged a reconstruction act.
Ye Gods! what inconsistency indeed,
What! reconstruct that which could not secede?
It knew the whites could never be controlled,
By mongrel views, or of their rights cajoled;
So for the negro it prepared the feast,
And drove him to the poll-box like a beast;
While carpetbaggers o'er him held the rod,
Through leagues more potent than the church of God.
'Gainst ev'ry interest of the South arrayed,
This party on its very vitals preyed;
Degrading schemes, disgusting to relate,
Were nurtured in the mansion of the state,
From there diffused in every garb and form,
They swept the country like a Siroc's storm.

Ah! Nature's blessings rest upon this land,
And here she strows her gifts with lavish hand,
Here fragrant flowers bloom along the lea,
And blushing fruits doth hang on every tree;
Here grassy vales and fleecy fields are seen,
Wide seas of golden grain and pastures green:
What charming verdure o'er its hills expand!
Yet man would ruin all with spiteful hand.
O Heaven when will thy fierce vengeance scourge,
Away the plague and this bright region purge?
Of all that mars thy brightest gifts divine,
And let thy beams once more upon us shine,
Thy smiles disperse the low'ring clouds of woe,
And peace and freedom on this land bestow.

Relieve it of that grim and cumbrous load,
Which balks its progress and blocks every road
That leads to peace, prosperity and wealth,
And poisons every stream and source of health.

The polls were opened to one million men,
Who knew nor letter nor a scratch of pen;
And whose untutor'd thoughts had never steered,
Above the cotton and the corn they reared;
Who owned no property, yet in their hand,
They siezed the reins of state and ruled the land;
And shaped its laws to suit the robber's will,
And at his mercy placed the public till:
While heroes were from every right debarred,
And rebels, traitors and outlaws declared;
Were heaped with insult by that rabble horde,
Who never dared to stand before their sword.

'Twas best to die amid the cannons' roar,
On famed Potomac's fair and classic shore;
Or by the Rapidan's historic flood,
Where countless heroes spilt their noble blood.
On Shilo's plains where gallant JOHNSTON fell,
While his fierce lines were sweeping hill and dell;
Where his last view and fading vision saw,
His troops achieve the mightiest feats of war;
And without thought of self or war's alarms,
He gently fell to sleep in glory's arms:
Exclaiming, while his gaze was fixed upon
His charging columns, "Was not that well done?"
We have them now, and ere the nightfall we
Will drink the waters of the Tennessee.
He saw the goal, he stood upon the mount,
But ere the evening, drank at Heaven's fount.

Or on that war-clad mountain's rugged side,
Where noble POLK, the mitred hero died:
Mid altars, courts and camps, where e'er he moved,
He was by church and state and army loved.
Ah! let him rest beneath the soldiers' sod,
For well he served his country and his God.

Ye flow'ry vales! where flows the Cumb'rland's tide,
On your red lap a noble patriot died;
Ye can to fame a splendid tribute bring,
Its echoes waft the story of Mill-Spring;
Where e'er the muse the hero's page unfold,
The death of ZOLLICOFFER will be told.

Missouri has her blazing altars too
Of glory, kindled by her brave and true:
Who fought with PRICE, M'CULLOUGH and VAN DORN,
Amid the fiery billows of Elk-Horn.
'Twas there M'CULLOUGH met his daring death,
Amid the vortex of red battle's breath:
And gallant Texas lost a jewel there,
That added luster to her brilliant star.
Alas! ye "comrades of the Southern Cross,"
Too well you know the compass of your loss,
When your brave CLEBURN found the soldier's rest,
The firery STONEWALL JACKSON of the West.
Your azure flag to Federals, so well known,
Was never more on path of victory borne.
Ah! let his ashes rest in glory's urn,
The torch he kindled will forever burn.

And who were found the shining roll to fill,
Of dashing STEWART and the veteran HILL?

Virginia! Mother whom I love so well,
Two jewels more from your bright garland fell.
They fell; their country reaped a mortal wound,
And to grim fate's stern chariot wheel was bound.
Ah! sound fame's trumpet, let the welkin ring,
No muse can truly of their glory sing;
No pantomime display their brilliant parts,
Their deeds are tuned upon their people's hearts.
Their names will glitter on historic page,
And brighten as they pass from age to age.

The *rebel* dead, the glorious *rebel* dead,
No dub of hate can bow their country's head;
Beyond the shafts of death or hatred's ban,
Their names are safe, their deeds ennobled man:
They fell with honor in their country's fight,
With conscience basking in the beams of right.
Whatever be their cause or right or wrong,
They live in Heaven, in history and in song;
Their tents are spread on glory's verdant *grave*,
The Campus Martius of eternal fame.

OUR CONFEDERATE DEAD.

Dulce est pro patria mori.